A Nation of
Haters and Victims

Or a Nation of Thinkers, Hopers, and Doers

RUTH E. TODD

iUniverse, Inc.
New York   Bloomington

iUniverse books may be ordered through booksellers or by contacting:

iUniverse
1663 Liberty Drive
Bloomington, IN 47403
www.iuniverse.com
1-800-Authors (1-800-288-4677)

ISBN: 978-1-4502-0613-6 (pbk)
ISBN: 978-1-4502-0614-3 (ebk)

Library of Congress Control Number: 2010900331

Printed in the United States of America

iUniverse rev. date: 2/08/2010

Contents

Preface

This tome is short by design. I did not want to try to historically document every event that could have further proven the case that we are increasingly becoming a nation of haters and victims and victims turned haters and haters turned victims. My only sources were the media and my memory. I thank my family for helping me see the haters and victims and for encouraging me to write and tell the story as I see it. I have been an observer of history most of my life. I have also used academic pursuits to further my love of history. I hold an MA in history and an MBA in global management, but nothing in my education prepared me for either the events I document in this book or the realization of what we need to do to fix the problem.

The Beginning

The United States is a unique country. It was founded by those who wanted to escape state-sponsored religions and political oppression. It was born of the philosophies of Rousseau, Locke, Paine, and Hume. It also arose from thinking, discourse, and dissent—always with an eye to what could be built and not just what could be torn down. This seemed to work for many years, but recently there has been a blight affecting many in this country. In the last two decades there has seemed to be a rush to judgment. Duke Lacrosse players, a congressman from California, a basketball player—all could be guilty of something, but before investigations are complete and the facts known, haters and victims foment misinformation and hate. Now is the time to take stock of who we are and who we want to be, and to make sure that we are more akin to the thinkers than the haters.

We seem to be at a crossroads. Which way will we go? Will we move toward the future or mire ourselves in conspiracies and distrust? Haters and victims are ready to continue their dark arts, but thinkers, hopers, and doers can still win the war. The whole world is waiting for the answer, as what we do here affects them as well.

Adolf Hitler wrote, "How fortunate for governments that people they administer do not think." It is not just the government that is fortunate; it is also all of the haters and victims who continuously preach the gospel of hatred and victimhood. The United States has been infected by a disease that taints all that we do. Haters and victims have permeated our society and created a national malaise that makes us unable to think clearly.

It is time for us to think for ourselves. Sound bites and filtered information that appeal to our emotions have gone on long enough. We need to do our own research to discover the truth of things. This nation was built by men and women who had vision, forethought, wisdom, and dreams. While we cannot point to every event in our history with pride, as a nation we have made great strides in creating an environment for growth and equality. We are an experiment that succeeded, and while not perfect, it is the envy of many. In the press, you hear about those who preach about taking the country back. If you want to do this, take it back from the haters and victims. Think! Because we stopped thinking for ourselves and allowed others to tell us what to think, our national character has been altered—but it is not too late. If we want to be cured, we must acknowledge the problem. Failure to think and reason caused the extermination of Native Americans, discrimination in employment for immigrants, Jim Crow laws, and black codes (laws that limited the civil rights of African Americans). But we are not so far removed from these events that we cannot learn from our mistakes and move forward.

The United States is undoubtedly the nation most other countries love to hate, but many people around the world ignore this tendency and choose to love us anyway. We have for centuries offered hope to people who have been oppressed and downtrodden. Colonists came here seeking a better life and wanting freedom from the state-sponsored religions of Europe. The United States is a country whose people built a government, economy, and lifestyle that have become the envy of the world. This is all to our credit, but there is a disease affecting us. It is not AIDS; it is not H1N1; it is not cancer. This sickness is uglier than those, and for the nation it is much more damaging. We have allowed haters and victims to alter how we think of our country, ourselves, and our neighbors.

Fearmongering and hatemongering have become full-time jobs for many in this country. Not only are people profiting from this business; they are causing irreparable harm to this nation. I am not speaking of comedians who take the darker things and poke at them so we find humor in our folly, but the haters who keep telling us how bad things are and who is to blame, as well as those who think they are victims.

There are haters and there are victims, and there are those haters who become victims and so-called victims who become haters. This dark circle is somehow convinced that they do not control their own destinies and that other people get special treatment. They assume that what they hear on talk radio is what the truth is. They also assume that things they read on Internet sites are true without verifying who the owner/sponsor of the Web site is.

These people say they want our president to fail while they wave the flag and call themselves Americans. They call black people racists while insisting that they are not themselves racists and maintain that there is a level playing field for minorities. They also stretch the truth or speak half-truths, and when they are called to account for the words they have uttered, they hide under the cover of First Amendment rights, which they think only apply to them, not to those who don't reek of malicious intent.

Besides the fact that there is a great deal of money to be made by being vicious and reducing our nation to the level of the debauched and decayed Roman Empire—with everything becoming like the public entertainment in the Coliseum—haters and victims are not the watchers and keepers of the flame. Instead, they are the destroyers of dreams and hope. *Quis custodiet ipsos custodes?* (Who watches the watchers?) People in the haters' and victims' group want no scrutiny for their actions and want to be free to criticize everyone else in the most hateful terms.

The Hater and Victim Fear

Fear is not rational. It is an emotional response to something that makes us feel concern for our safety and well-being. Haters and victims will attack groups whose only mission is to champion our rights under the constitution, such as the American Civil Liberties Union. They fear antidefamation leagues because these groups use education and information to defeat the lies and half-truths that feed haters and victims. Associations such as the American Association of Retired People can be vilified for trying to protect some of the most vulnerable among us, the seniors. The Department of Justice is "out to get us": yes, government agents have made mistakes, but these seem to be errors in judgment and not government policy. Agencies such as the United Nations, the World Bank, and the International Monetary Fund are frightening to the haters and victims; they, too, are "out to get us." The North American Free Trade Agreement (NAFTA) and other free trade agreements seem to show the victims and haters that no one is looking out for them. They would have us build walls along our borders and somehow stop globalization and free markets. That boat has left the dock, and there is no turning back. Since one tribe first discovered other tribes, trade has existed, and globalization is the extension of centuries of trade.

The Awareness of Haters and Victims

I was born and raised in Chicago, and I came of age in the 1960s. My mother owned a restaurant in a blue-collar neighborhood filled with small businesses, manufacturing sites, apartments, and some homes. Chicago is a phenomenal city loaded with diversity, and if the United States is a melting pot, then Chicago is Melting Pot Central. My mother's customers were a collage of races, genders, religions, ethnicities, and economic classes. Southern blacks, Asians, Haitians, Jamaicans, Mexicans, Cubans, Jews, Puerto Ricans, Trinidadians, Africans, Native Americans, Appalachian whites, middle-class Caucasians, and professional people, such as lawyers, factory owners, and insurance executives, all were customers.

I frequently say that I was unaware of the haters and victims when I was growing up around this restaurant. The idea that there were people who hated based on skin color or ethnic origin was foreign to me. The idea that there were people who constantly claimed that their problems stemmed from others who were somehow advantaged when they themselves were not was also foreign to me. There were no differences in our customer base to me; they all were customers. They provided me with an education in religions, races, cultures, languages, governments, and why people came to the United States. If victims and haters came in, I was unaware of them. There could have been some there, but the audience was not receptive to their message and the media were not so dedicated to making people hate and feel like victims.

When I was growing up, we read newspapers and listened to radio, and there seemed to be standards for what could and could not be printed or broadcast. Radio was a medium for entertainment and sports; there were few talk shows, and the news shows reported the news. I remember election results being reported in terms of numbers, not in terms of red states and blue states. I remember when the idea of shock radio was a Beatles song. I remember the antiwar protests and the emotion and rhetoric directed to ending the war. When Nixon resigned, I remember a nation disillusioned by his actions, and while there was a smattering of invective heaped on the man, it was tame compared to the daily diatribe flung at anyone in public office today. The Reagan years were the years when I became keenly aware of the victims and haters. The Strategic Defense Initiative (SDI), better known as Star Wars, the firing of the air traffic controllers, the continued deregulation of industries, and the constant drone of patriotic propaganda were the hallmark of these years.

Here was a popular president who used every political trick in the book to remain popular. His reliance on Cold War rhetoric, well-placed sound bites, and huge budget deficits became topics of argument. If you were not a Reaganite, there was something wrong with you. Heated discussions soon became opportunities for attacks on you, not on his policies. I thought it was a phase or part of a cycle the nation was experiencing, like the McCarthy era, but it never went away. The nation did not grow out of this phase; instead, it grew worse. The person running for the presidency or elected to the presidency became a target for every sort of loathing from the victims and haters.

The more I became aware of this blight that was infecting us the more I began listening and observing. I spent many hours wondering if our nation had always been so negative and ugly. I looked into history and found that our role models in Europe had little to offer us in the way of moderation and compassion. The Spanish Inquisition was a particularly low point in history. Europe had made primogeniture the law of the land. It invented the feudal system to trap peasants. There was no universal education. The law favored landowners and they were the ones who introduced slavery into the New World. The European conquerors certainly showed us how to decimate native populations so the conquerors could acquire their land and resources.

Then I thought about the persecution of the Tories, the forced removal of the Cherokees, and the tainted *Dred Scott* and *Plessey v. Ferguson* Supreme Court decisions. While these actions may have been misdirected and deplorable, they did not seem to be part of the nation's evolving identity and we seemed to be following a pattern in history. For the most part, we recorded and studied these events, but today we have added a new twist in recording events.

We now have an inordinate number of screamers and loud, vocal media types who have snake venom in their veins, and this venom flows out of their mouths. We have Rush Limbaugh, Glenn Beck, Michael Savage, and Sean Hannity ensuring that hatred and victimhood continue. There are others, but these men have shown that they are more openly preaching the gospel of hate and victimhood than others. Their bottom line is, "If you tell a lie often enough you can make it the truth." In some cases they use words used by Paine and others as part of a title of rants they publish so they can gain some modicum of credibility, however weak.

I have watched documentaries from the 1940s, 1950s, and 1960s, and the haters then seemed to exist in small groups. Over the past four or five decades, we seem to have had an epidemic of haters and victims, and this is not to our collective national advantage. The more we hate, the more we fear, and the more we fear, the more we hate.

Ordinary people are afraid, but they are uncertain about what they fear. They seem to be aligned with Thomas Hobbes and his quote, "Life is nasty, brutish, and short." This idea is alien to most of us, and if asked as individuals, we would indicate some happiness and optimism, but the negativity seems to be the collective thinking of the pack. People are afraid because they have been told to be afraid: of immigration and trade agreements and change. The basis for this fear is anchored in quicksand, but still they must be afraid. In the absence of common sense, education, and personal reflection, the message of hate and victim carries the day. What is little understood is that America is not easy. If you want freedom of speech, than it must apply to all who live here. If you want freedom of the press, than it it must apply to all press.

Manifestation of Haters and Victims

We seem to have lost the ability to trust, respect, and have a meaningful discourse with others. At the first hint of resistance, we shout epithets, initiate confrontations, and in loud voices spew unresolved wrongs out of our mouths. Every action is twisted and turned so even good begins to look bad. Allegations, innuendos, secret agendas, and conspiracies dog our days and blare from televisions. Americans are told to be afraid of terrorists and immigrants and the government. Someone has to tell people who to be afraid of and who the cause of their problems is.

Terror alerts are just one visible piece of how people are manipulated and told to be afraid. Look under the bed and see if someone is hiding there. This is akin to the Communist bogeyman of the 1950s. Someone is going to take our jobs. Some undesirable is going to want our homes or will want to marry our daughters. Everyone is out to get us. We look for slights, insults, and misdeeds. And if we look for these things, we will find them.

For many, everything is personal. Some of us have come to believe that people do things to us and we are the injured parties. We are angry and increasingly hateful, spiteful, and violent. We have become a nation of litigants, proving our victimhood. Some of these litigations are justified, but many are not. We constantly want to make sure we get what is, in our opinion, rightfully ours. We never seem to be satisfied, and we wonder what someone has done for us lately because we have already forgotten yesterday. We carry this invisible bag of wrongs and slights, and when it is full we dump it all over others, even if they were not the cause for the bag being filled.

This victimhood of many Americans extends even to the tobacco industry and the stated victims of cigarette smoking. To the best of my knowledge, no one ever forced anyone to buy cigarettes, light them, and smoke them. While the tobacco companies are culpable for creating entertaining advertising and ensuring that the amount of nicotine and additives in cigarettes would keep smokers smoking, the people accountable for smoking are the smokers. The current climate does not allow for this reasoning, however.

The haters and victims assassinated John Kennedy, Robert Kennedy, Medgar Evers, Malcolm X, and Martin Luther King Jr. This list is not complete. Victims elect people to office who often reflect their own level of misinformation and ignorance; somehow they think these politicians will look out for their constituents' interests more than their own. The proof of this was clearly shown in the 2000 election in Florida. Never was it clearer that there was a need for caution about those we elect to local and state government because when we elect people who rise to their own level of mediocrity, we will certainly not be satisfied with our choices.

We talk about immigrants as if immigrant were a four-letter word, and most of us seem to have forgotten that our own citizenship is a gift from those who immigrated here earlier. We live with misinformation and promote chain e-mails that are lies, and if a lie is repeated often enough it becomes the truth. Minorities, gays, lesbians, Native Americans, non-Christians, and women are all groups receiving the opprobrium of the haters and victims. Tolerance and justice are forgotten. Hate, violence, discrimination, prejudice, and bigotry mark our days.

How did this happen? When did it happen? Does it have to continue? Why did it happen?

History is littered with the many tales of fear and hate running amok. The Salem witch trials, the Trail of Tears, segregation, discrimination, the treatment of new immigrants, the murder of Joseph Smith, the Ku Klux Klan, and the internment of the Japanese during World War II are all examples. There are also some examples that bear retelling. This short book will document many examples of haters and victims at work. I certainly cannot document all, but I will list some that demonstrate the vilest deeds of haters and victims. I will also offer recommendations for how this nation can pull itself back from the abyss of intolerance.

Leo Frank

Although I may not have been aware of the haters, when I was younger, there is evidence of their existence. In 1913, Leo Frank was convicted of murdering Mary Phagan. Mary was a thirteen-year-old employee of an Atlanta pencil factory where Frank was the manager. He was also Jewish. Frank was found guilty of the crime but after Georgia's governor commuted his death sentence, a mob stormed the prison where Frank was being held and lynched him. Leo Frank thus became the only known Jew lynched in American history. The evidence did not point to Frank as the murderer, and he was not placed at the scene of the crime, but the mob did not care; they cared that he was a Jew and that made him guilty. Whoever killed Mary was never caught and certainly never punished. The mob had spoken on behalf of the haters and victims. This is what happens when we fail to think. Innocent people die, and guilty people are never brought to justice.

Freedom Riders

The Freedom Riders were some of the early and courageous pioneers in the battle for racial equality. Their journey began on May 4, 1961. Thirteen young people, seven blacks and six whites, left Washington DC to force desegregation of public transportation in the South. By the second week of the journey, the Riders had been severely beaten. Near Anniston, Alabama, one of their buses was burned. In Birmingham, the Riders were attacked by several dozen white people just two short blocks away from the sheriff's office. The Freedom Riders were viciously attacked by more than a thousand whites outside Montgomery, Alabama, but they continued to Mississippi, where they endured more violence and brutality. The federal government reinforced the desegregation ruling mandated by the Supreme Court's *Brown vs. Board of Education* decision, and enabled by the Freedom Riders' bravery, protest spread to train stations and airports throughout the South. The haters tried to stop this from happening, but the desire for change and the number of people willing to fight for it were greater than the population of haters.

Lunch Counter Sit-ins

On February 1, 1960, four North Carolina college students did something brave. They sat down at a Woolworth lunch counter in Greensboro, North Carolina, and waited for service. While the students knew that most likely they would not be served, they were also aware that this form of nonviolent protest was potentially a powerful method to desegregate lunch counters. This was not the first lunch counter sit-in. The first had occurred 1943 in Chicago, and others had been held in Baltimore and St. Louis; now, though, the focus was on the southern states.

On the first day of the sit-in, the students arrived at the Woolworth store in the afternoon. They took seats at the lunch counter and encountered silence from the white patrons. At first, servers ignored them and then they were told that they would not be served. They sat quietly and waited. When the police chief was notified, he informed the store management that nothing could be done as long as the students were peaceful. Since the police refused to remove the students and the students would not budge, the store closed early. The students left with the intent to return the following day. Woolworth store management had decided they would rather have no business than publicly serve someone of color.

After the first day, word about the sit-in spread in the community. The following day, two more students joined the original group. The media picked up the story, and over the next several days the protestors were joined by more students, including whites. The effectiveness of the sit-ins was due in part to the behavior of the participants. They dressed in their Sunday clothes and were quiet, nonviolent, and respectful. Many students brought their textbooks and read and studied while they sat at the lunch counters.

The sit-in movement spread to other cities. Prior to the Greensboro sit-in, Nashville students had been preparing and training for sit-ins, and the Nashville, Tennessee, community quickly joined the movement. Their training had been designed to limit the potential for violence: passive resistance was the mantra of this movement, and when it was their turn, they were ready. On February 13, 1960, around five hundred students participated in the first Nashville sit-in. They organized into groups and went downtown to Woolworth, Kresge's, McCellan's, and other stores. On the first day and for several more days, they did not encounter any violence. Then things changed. On February 27, white teenagers attacked the student protestors. When the police arrived, they let the white teens go and arrested the sit-in protesters for disorderly conduct.

The violence in Nashville continued. On April 19, the home of black attorney Z. Alexander Looby was destroyed by a bomb. Looby had been targeted because he represented the arrested student protestors. Luckily, Looby and his wife only suffered minor injuries. In response to the bombing and other violence, students and community members marched to City Hall. When they arrived they were greeted by Mayor Ben West. Fisk University student Diane Nash supported the protest, and she took the opportunity to ask the mayor if he thought it was right for lunch counters to discriminate based on race. West replied that, no, it was wrong. The next day, his statement was reported in the newspaper, and on May 10, six lunch counters in Nashville began serving black patrons.

Many young people today do not know of the bravery of the Freedom Riders or those who led the lunch counter sit-ins or why they were important, but they should.

Jane Fonda—
Celebrity Dissent

I have never met Jane Fonda but I have certainly read about her. She is an accomplished actor from a family of accomplished actors and has played many parts on and off the stage. She has also been dragged over the coals frequently because, during an unpopular time and an unpopular war, she exercised her rights as an American. Jane Fonda went to North Vietnam. Her actions there were ill-advised but this was her method of protesting the war. Her critics claimed she gave comfort to the enemy and did a disservice to American military personnel. I can understand why some may feel that way. I would posit that she actually demonstrated what separates the United States from dictatorships and repressive regimes around the world.

I do not agree with what she did and I would not have done it, but as an American she demonstrated her dislike for the war in a very public way, making use of her celebrity status. The notoriety surrounding her actions has certainly given the haters something to feed on even though the war has been over for more than thirty years. Somehow doing something very American became un-American.

A parallel case is Vanessa Redgrave. She was a vocal advocate for Palestine when it was equally unpopular to do so. Her acting career seems to have suffered as a result of her support because haters deemed her an anti-Semite. There are other examples of this kind of activity, but the message is clear. Even if you are a celebrity, you are subject to censorship, and the hate and victim mill grinds away. More recent examples would include Bruce Springsteen and the Dixie Chicks.

Voting Rights

During both the Kennedy and Johnson administrations, the Department of Justice was aware that many states would not allow blacks and other minorities to vote. This right was already granted under the Fifteenth Amendment, but some states ignored the Constitution. The murder of three voting-rights activists in Philadelphia, Mississippi, gained national attention, and the next move was to get blacks to vote, guarantee that they could, and ensure that their votes would be counted.

In Mississippi and Alabama, peaceful protestors were met with trained guard dogs and fire hoses. Jeering crowds, threats, and intimidations created a crescendo down streets lined with the faces of haters. A cacophony of hateful name-calling was broadcast around the world. The bullies had no shame. They took pride in beating people, spitting on little girls, bombing churches, and in some cases putting on sheets—because cowards need anonymity.

Acts of violence and terrorism were committed against blacks who attempted to register to vote and whites who supported their right to do so. Then on March 7, 1965, state troopers attacked peaceful marchers crossing the Edmund Pettus Bridge in Selma, Alabama, en route to the state capitol in Montgomery. President Johnson and Congress could not wait any longer, so they worked to overcome Southern legislators' resistance to effective voting rights legislation. President Johnson issued a call for a strong voting rights law, and hearings began soon thereafter on the bill that would become the Voting Rights Act of 1965.

In each of these stories, it is important to remember that the protests were all nonviolent. The protestors were attacked, beaten, and in some cases murdered, and the reason for the attacks was that they were exercising their right to protest. They did nothing to provoke the attacks, but attacked they were.

It is difficult for me to remember these events and the passage of the Voting Rights Act of 1965 and then compare them to the argument that the playing field had been leveled so the act did not need renewal in 1985 and 2005. According to sociologists, cultural changes take a minimum of two generations to become accepted into the society experiencing the change, and we simply did not all start at the same time. The hills are less steep today, but there is not yet a level playing field for women and minorities.

The Murder of
Emmett Till

Emmett Till left Chicago on August 20, 1955, to visit relatives in Money, Mississippi. He was fourteen years old and full of teenage bravado, a young black teen with little knowledge of Southern culture. He went to visit a tiny cotton gin town on the eastern edge of the Mississippi Delta. His mutilated corpse would return to Chicago in a coffin less than two weeks later.

Emmett was staying with his great uncle, Mose Wright. Mr. Wright was a sharecropper. The rural town of Money had only fifty-five residents, a gas station, and a grocery store. This was much different from urban Chicago, and the biggest difference was its racial climate: white people in Tallahatchie County, Mississippi, vigorously enforced Jim Crow segregation laws.

Racial tension in Mississippi ran high in August 1955 for many reasons but one of them was that just a few months earlier the US Supreme Court had ordered that southern states must integrate black students into white schools "with all deliberate speed." Many white people in the South felt that the Court and groups like the National Association for the Advancement of Colored People (NAACP) were attacking their way of life. Many were not interested in integration in schools, or buses, or restaurants or anywhere. Violence against blacks increased all over Mississippi, and several murders and beatings had already occurred in the area before Emmett came to visit.

On Wednesday, August 24, Emmett, his cousins, and some local kids were hanging out on the front porch of Bryant's Grocery and Meat Market playing checkers, listening to music, and telling stories. While talking about life up North, Emmett showed off some photographs and joked that a white girl in one picture was his girlfriend. One of the boys in the group laughed and said that there was a pretty white woman in the store and suggested he get a date with her. The boy's challenge stunned the others because they knew the dangers of a black male talking to a white woman—and asking a white woman on a date was unthinkable! But Emmett had no comprehension of the severe penalties inflicted on blacks who broke Jim Crow laws in the South, and he walked into the store while the kids outside crowded against the windows to see what would happen. When he left the store a few minutes later, witnesses reported that he turned, said "Bye, baby," and whistled the two-note "wolf whistle" at the white woman who worked behind the counter. News of the Chicago boy's crazy stunt zipped through the county like lightning, and by the time Roy Bryant, the woman's husband, returned from a road trip three days later, everyone in Tallahatchie County had heard the story. When Bryant heard it, he decided he and his half-brother, J. W. Milam, had to punish Emmett for being disrespectful to his wife. The two men planned to meet around 2:00 AM on Sunday to "teach the boy a lesson."

Mose Wright told reporters what happened next. "Sunday morning about two-thirty, someone came to the door. I asked who it was and he said, 'This is Mr. Bryant. I want to talk with you and the boy.'" When he opened the door, there was a man standing with a pistol in one hand and a flashlight in the other. Bryant and Milam forced their way into the back bedroom where Emmett was sleeping, and after making sure he was the one who had talked to Bryant's wife, they marched him outside to their car. That was the last time anyone in his family saw Emmett Till alive.

To the surprise of many people in the South, less than a day after Emmett's disappearance, authorities from Tallahatchie County and nearby Leflore County arrested Roy Bryant and J. W. Milam and charged them with kidnapping. Both men admitted they had taken the boy from his great-uncle's home but claimed they had turned him loose, unharmed, that same night. Three days later, a fisherman found Emmett Till's naked, battered body in the Tallahatchie River, and law enforcement officials then added murder to the charges against Roy Bryant and J. W. Milam.

A week after the two men's arrest, an all-white Sumner County grand jury surprised many when it ordered Bryant and Milam to stand trial for the murder of Emmett Till. But it was no surprise to most that the men were then acquitted of the murder in spite of the nature of the crime and pictures of the brutalized body that were publicized. Justice had not yet found a way to defeat the haters.

The Assassination of Medgar Evers

Medgar Evers was a civil rights leader and a field worker for the NAACP. He was assassinated in his driveway in Jackson, Mississippi, shot to death by a white supremacist, Byron De La Beckwith. Prior to his death, Evers had volunteered for the US Army and served in World War II, participating in the Normandy invasion. In 1952, he joined the NAACP. Evers traveled throughout his home state of Mississippi encouraging poor African Americans to register to vote and recruited them into the civil rights movement. He was instrumental in getting witnesses and evidence for the Emmitt Till murder case, which brought national attention to the lives and deaths of African Americans in the South. He himself was murdered on June 12, 1963.

After a funeral in Jackson, he was buried with full military honors at Arlington National Cemetery in Virginia. President John F. Kennedy and other leaders publicly condemned the senseless killing. His murder was more than just an assassination; it was also a travesty of justice. In 1964, the first trial of chief suspect Byron De La Beckwith ended with a deadlock by an all-white jury, sparking numerous protests. When a second all-white jury also failed to reach a decision, De La Beckwith was set free. Three decades later, the state of Mississippi reopened the case under pressure from civil rights leaders and the Evers family. In February 1994, a racially mixed jury in Jackson found Beckwith guilty of murder. The unrepentant white supremacist, aged seventy-three, was sentenced to life imprisonment.

Medgar was assassinated because he was trying to change a corrupt and bigoted system. His audience was the African Americans of

Mississippi who had not been allowed to register to vote. The murderer could not see that the blacks in Mississippi were citizens of the United States who should be afforded the rights of American citizens. This killer struck down the person who was helping lead the way because he could not strike out at all of them. He would have if he could have, but instead he struck out against a visible target whom he considered a threat.

The Assassination of JFK

John Fitzgerald Kennedy was the Democratic nominee for president in 1960. As soon as he was nominated, the smoldering haters and cynics appeared. The press published stories maintaining that because Kennedy was Catholic, if he were elected the pope would run the country. When this failed to take root, they looked for other bizarre stories to spread. This scheme was not successful, however, because he was elected president.

Kennedy was elected to office and served for just a thousand days. He was assassinated on November 22, 1963. Who the assassin was and why the assassin was willing to kill the president will probably never be known with certainty. But whoever it was, the motive is clear: Kennedy had made someone hate him enough to want him gone. It could have been Lee Harvey Oswald, or a disgruntled Cuban, or the mob, but no matter; the result was the death of a young, vibrant husband, father, and politician. He had campaigned on the theme of hope and promise, and then he was taken.

This president was not perfect, but for a brief time he offered optimism, hope, goals, and a future to a nation shell-shocked by the Cold War and desperately wanting to look to the future. I remember how vibrant he seemed and how people responded to his message of hope. I remember how the nation mourned his passing.

The Assassination of Martin Luther King Jr.

Martin Luther King Jr. was a minister who energized the civil rights movement and became the embodiment of social justice. He knew the task was dangerous, but he was able to build a coalition of Catholics and Jews, whites and blacks, rich and poor, famous and unknown. He led marches, made speeches, and inspired a nation to make great changes. There were many who feared such changes and thought that minorities would somehow claim all that others owned. They did not understand—or simply did not want to understand—that the goal was equal footing and equal rights.

In the months before his assassination, King became increasingly concerned with the problem of economic inequality in America. This concern moved his activities from only civil rights to social activism. He planned an interracial "Poor People's March" on Washington. In March 1968, King traveled to Memphis to support poorly paid and poorly treated African American sanitation workers. On March 28, a workers' protest march led by King ended in violence and the death of an African American teenager. King left the city but vowed to return in early April to lead more demonstrations. The violence had been initiated by the onlookers, not the protestors. Fear and fear of change won the day.

King returned to Memphis to support the sanitation workers' strike. Just after 6:00 PM on April 4, 1968, he was fatally shot while standing on the balcony outside his second-story room at the Motel Lorraine in Memphis, Tennessee. The civil rights leader was on his way to dinner when a bullet struck him in the jaw and severed his spinal cord. Just thirty-nine years old, he was pronounced dead after his arrival at a Memphis hospital. Once again a father, husband, and leader was struck down much too soon.

The Assassination
of Malcolm X

On February 21, 1965, Malcolm X was assassinated as he began to address a rally in New York City. He was a controversial figure, but he was also charismatic, committed, dedicated, and outspoken. He had spent time in jail for crimes associated with inner-city living. While in prison he converted to Islam, and after leaving prison he eventually became a spokesman for Elijah Mohammed's Nation of Islam. Initially, he articulated and promoted a blatantly anti-white program of black self-help.

The phrase he used, which made others feel like haters and potential victims, was "by any means necessary." These words energized those who were afraid of civil rights, afraid of black people, or afraid that their jobs were threatened. Perhaps they were afraid like the slave owners who survived the Nat Turner rebellion had been in years past.

After a trip to Mecca, Malcolm X broke with Elijah Muhammad and his anti-white policies to form an independent political group addressing both national and international concerns. His changed views put him at odds with Elijah Muhammad, and he knew his life was in danger. He had received death threats, his home had been fire-bombed, and there had been shots fired before. Finally, on that February day, someone was successful: he was shot as he addressed a gathering in a Harlem ballroom. A young black man named Thomas Hagan was charged with the killing. The police rescued Hagan from the outraged crowd after he had been shot and beaten. An autopsy showed that Malcolm had been shot by more than one gun and more than one caliber of bullet; Hagan had not acted alone.

The Assassination of Robert Francis Kennedy

On June 4, 1968, Senator Robert F. Kennedy had just won the all-important California primary, and as the Democratic Party looked to its convention, it was assured that he would be its presidential nominee. He had just spoken at the ballroom of a Los Angeles hotel, thanking his supporters and saying, "Now on to Chicago," the site of the 1968 Democratic National Convention. Shots rang out and Kennedy was hit. He died a few hours later, early on the morning of June 5. Like his brother, he had enemies. Exactly who they were and why they struck is really unknown, but the fact remains that someone hated him and feared him so much that he killed him. A man was arrested and convicted of the crime but it is still unclear why he would do this dark deed. Yet again, a young vibrant, articulate, father, husband, and politician was struck down. It appeared the haters were winning. I remember watching this bizarre and sad event over and over on the television. So many assassinations, so many good people lost.

The Cold War

The Cold War was a defining period in both world history and US history. Starting after the Allied victory in World War II, it was the ultimate game of chicken. Real weapons of mass destruction, the MAD (mutually assured destruction) theory, and the Hot Line were the hallmarks of our daily lives. On the surface, the country was experiencing an economic boom; homes were built, the suburbs sprouted up, and the steel mills were working three shifts a day. Life was good, but the man behind the curtain was not unknown: he was the shadow of a nuclear world war, and no one would win it. We did not want to look behind the curtain because fear and thoughts of nuclear destruction were there, and we did not want to uncork that bottle.

The haters and victims were well represented in the personage of Joseph McCarthy. An expert in spreading fear, he was an opportunist who sought his moments of fame by accusing almost everyone from the president to actors to teachers of being communists. McCarthy had ordinary people looking under their beds and in their closets for communists. He encouraged citizens to spy on their neighbors. We wanted the American way of life to continue, but some allowed fear to change how we looked at people and what they said. The First Amendment was under siege. Because we were afraid, we needed someone to blame and McCarthyism took root.

The Korean Conflict added to our fear. This was our first taste of a war we did not win. Flush with victory from the end of World War II, we faced the harsh reality of Korea in doubt about our abilities, and we feared that other nations had the ability to attack us. Concern and paranoia grew in some parts of the population. Ordinary people had faith that they would be unaffected by the events occurring so far away and that the government was able to protect their interests, but there was a population that had no such faith.

This psychology became even more evident during the Cuban Missile Crisis. Khrushchev, the Soviet leader, was testing our mettle and thought he would find us wanting. Well, we did not back down and while we feared that JFK was an inexperienced president whom Khrushchev could bully, this did not happen: the missiles left Cuba. But then the president was assassinated, and our foreign policy was linked to the domino theory and not letting all of Vietnam fall to the communists; it was believed that if Vietnam fell, so would Japan and the rest of Southeast Asia, just as China had already fallen.

So what had been a civil war in a small Southeast Asian country became a conflict draining resources and lives from America and a few allies. This time our involvement was questioned. There was not a clear explanation of why we needed to be there. The civil rights movement had given people a voice, and other voices were also joining in the chorus. Women, Hispanics, and Asians became part of a visible and growing group that clamored for change, and these voices frequently joined with the anti–Vietnam War movement. Many Americans never understood this conflict.

The other problem was the politicians of this era. They not only wanted to run the war, they did run it. No war has been run well when managed by politicians. The lesson we should have learned is to let the military run the strategy as they were actually trained to do. If they fail, you replace them, but at least you have the experts on the matter running the war.

Vietnam became the poster child for failed foreign policy. Americans picked sides, probably much as they did during the American Civil War. If you were not for the war, then you were against it, and being against the war made you un-American. It was the beginning of pitting one group against another group and siblings against each other. Divided we fall.

The War on Poverty

The War on Poverty is another lightning rod for haters and victims. First of all, you cannot have a war on poverty. This is political rhetoric and nothing more. War, by definition, is a state of usually open and declared armed hostile conflict between states or nations. Obviously, poverty does not qualify. The issue with this war is that it pitted the poor against the middle class and the poor against the wealthy. The demarcation lines between these groups became wider and more obvious. Every act, including food stamps, welfare, Medicaid, Head Start, and housing subsidies, became the focus of hate for some. Complaints about taxes masked the real issue. Someone was getting something that many felt was unearned and unwarranted, and this was accompanied by the idea that someone else was getting something they themselves could not get. The haters and victims appeared on the scene with diatribes to evoke the emotions of others. They repeatedly stated the problems, but had no answers.

The reasons for poverty were not eradicated. Hunger, lack of education, joblessness, discrimination, substandard housing, and lack of qualified medical care—both preventative and remedial—were not fixed. The wealthy complained about taxes, and their voices were heard. The middle class found themselves more like the monkey in the middle. They paid higher taxes but could not qualify for any relief, and they were told it was "those people" who were the cause of their problems.

For some Americans, every action in the civil rights movement was another indicator that they were victims or would become victims. Minority hiring programs, universities using quotas to get minorities admitted, the creation of the Equal Employment Opportunity Act, and even the Occupational Safety and Health Act were viewed not as ways to make us safer but as pandering to minorities and costing the middle class jobs. Some white men became concerned over the potential loss of jobs and equated this to threatening the white race.

The War on Drugs

The War on Drugs is a sham. The same comments apply here as they do to the War on Poverty. This so-called war has cost US taxpayers billions of dollars, and yet the drugs keep coming and the drug users keep using. Moreover, we have many ways to stop the flow of illegal drugs but our overstated sense of morality will not broach the cures. If we legalize and tax marijuana, we will not only generate hard revenue for the tax coffers around the country, we will also take a big prop out from under countries that take our money to fight the war and yet let the drugs flow into America in even greater tonnage. If we legalize marijuana, we could save millions of tax dollars on prisons as we could pardon the users and send this proportion of the prison population home. If this was done, it should be possible to keep the more serious criminals in jail.

The Netherlands has had legal drug use for several decades. They have reduced AIDS infections and crime, and collected taxes. The country has a robust economy and a firm commitment to civil liberties. Maybe we should dust off our credentials and see how we currently stack up. Maybe the victims and haters would find that the Patriot Act is a bigger danger to our way of life than the terrorists are—and certainly more dangerous than marijuana.

The War on Terror

We are three for three on this topic. We cannot win this war, at least not militarily. If we want to curb or eradicate terrorism, we must start with ourselves and we must stop being afraid. I do not dispute that 9/11 was a despicable act by desperate people who feared our way of life so much that they took extraordinary measures to impede our influence and harm our economy. The 9/11 terrorists were successful, but they do not have to continue to be so.

Terrorist states are predominately poor, uneducated, and underdeveloped, ruled by strongmen or a few rich families. These countries have little access to news from around the world, and they are told that the United States is harming them or attacking their religion or occupying their country and altering their culture, so they need to be soldiers. For many years those living behind the Iron Curtain were told how good they had it and how bad it was in the West. Pictures of the worst parts of our society were shown over and over to prove that point. For many it was an eye-opener to discover that our poorest Americans had more than most of their citizenry did.

On a trip to Russia several years ago, I was given a tour of some historic sites. The information the trained Russian tour guide had available was not completely accurate. I asked a few questions, and then the tour guide explained that he only knew what he was told and they were just finding out things they should have known. Knowledge is power. It is hard to keep people on the farm when they have seen Paris or London or San Francisco. It is even harder to keep them down when they are given access to books and training.

Technology, especially communications technology, is a vital and effective weapon in this battle. It is not a coincidence that Iran, North Korea, and other dictatorships have government-owned, -run and

-censored television, newspapers, and radio. We need to pay attention to this censorship because the media in the United States has become increasingly centralized over the last couple of decades and this is not a benefit to those who listen to the distorted reports. You can ensure the ignorance and hatred of the population by not exposing them to facts, dissent, or concepts not present in their own systems. Label them terrorists or communists or liberals and if that is the only story being told then this is all people will know. If we want to fight terrorism and the countries that breed it, we must fight it with information, education, and employment. If we want to win against the terrorists, we must show that we are not a nation divided by hate and fear.

The Los Angeles Riots

On April 29, 1992, a truck driver named Reginald Denny took a shortcut off an LA freeway. The Rodney King trial jury had just announced a verdict. Denny was unaware of what was happening in LA, and he drove into an area where a group of rioters were enraged over the verdict. As he crossed Florence, a group of angry people rushed toward him and pulled him out of the cab of his truck. He was severely beaten and his head was smashed by a cinderblock. His crime was simply that he was white, and that was all the haters needed to know at the time.

The story does have a twist that shows that not all haters win. Four South Central residents raced to the scene and, at some risk to themselves, grabbed Denny and drove him to a hospital, where doctors were able to save his life. And the story has another twist. Denny needed rehabilitative therapy for years, but he approached the families of the beaters in a gesture of forgiveness. Denny could have become a hater, something we all would have understood, but instead he chose forgiveness and peace.

Matthew Shepard

On November 4, 1999, a Wyoming man was sentenced to death for the murder of a gay college student named Matthew Shepard. Aaron McKinney and Russell Henderson had both been sentenced for the murder. Police testified that McKinney and his friend Henderson lured Shepard from a bar in Laramie, pistol-whipped him, tied him to a fence outside of town, and left him to die. Shepard, who was only twenty-one, was not found for some eighteen hours. He died five days later in a hospital at Fort Collins, Colorado, without regaining consciousness. Prosecutors said McKinney was like a "wolf" preying on his smaller victim. Defense lawyers argued that he never intended to kill Shepard—as if failure to have intent is compensation for deeds most foul.

The defense attorneys attempted to use a "gay panic" defense, based on the theory that some men are prone to an uncontrollable, violent reaction when propositioned by a homosexual. They told the court that McKinney was crazed by drugs and alcohol and flew into a blind rage when Shepard allegedly made an unwelcome sexual advance that revived memories of childhood sexual abuse. So it was the victim's fault that McKinney killed him because he was threatened by a young, slight, twenty-one-year-old gay man.

I am sure that two wrongs do not somehow make a right here, but what I see is yet another logical fallacy foisted off on the American people by defense attorneys whose single purpose, at least in this case, is to make guilty people look like victims and not haters. It was a good effort, but thankfully this jury could also see the horrific nature of the crime and judged accordingly.

James Byrd

In 1998, in the small town of Jasper, Texas, a forty-nine-year-old black man was dragged to death along a stretch of country road. In the early morning of June 7, three white men used a logging chain to tie James Byrd Jr.'s ankles to the rear bumper of a pickup truck. Byrd's remains were strewn throughout the stretch of Huff Creek Road and were eventually found in seventy-five different places. His keys were in one place, his dentures were in another, and his head and his right arm were discovered a mile from his torso. The crime shocked the nation and jolted the town of Jasper. This horrific murder was committed by Shawn Allen Berry, Lawrence Russell Brewer, and John William King. All were found guilty of the murder.

Why did they decide to commit this crime, and why James Byrd? There was talk about drugs and alcohol, and those certainly contributed, but there were also white supremacy and hate tattoos and a history of wanting to make sure they protected themselves from people like James Byrd. Byrd was in the wrong place at the wrong time, through no fault of his own.

Eric Rudolph

Eric Rudolph, a self-proclaimed member of the Army of God, had his own agenda of hate. He blamed his victims for his crimes—his perception of what he considered aberrant behavior on the part of gay people and legalized abortion were the stated reasons. This is yet another example of faulty logic. He felt compelled to take judgment into his hands, so he disrupted the Olympic Games in Atlanta in 1996 and bombed abortion clinics and a bar that served gay people. As a member of the Army of God, it did not occur to Rudolph that only God can judge us and determine our eternal fate. In his wake he left death, permanent disabilities, and destruction. After he has served his four consecutive life sentences he will be judged by the right Authority.

Timothy McVeigh

Timothy McVeigh looked like an ordinary young man, recently released from military service and trying to settle down somewhere. But looks can deceive. McVeigh was said to be angered by the Waco tragedy and decided to enact his own brand of retribution against the federal government, especially the FBI and the Bureau of Alcohol, Tobacco, and Firearms (ATF). In downtown Oklahoma City, the Alfred P. Murrah Federal Building held numerous federal agency offices, including those of the ATF. With the help of several like-minded people, McVeigh decided to act. He had served in the military, and for the task he had chosen he was well trained.

On April 17, 1995, McVeigh rented a Ryder truck. He and his friend Terry Nichols loaded it with approximately five thousand pounds of ammonium nitrate fertilizer. On the morning of April 19, McVeigh drove the Ryder truck to the Murrah Federal Building, lit the bomb's fuse, parked in front of the building, left the keys inside the truck, and locked the door. Then he walked across the parking lot to an alley and started to jog.

Most employees of the Murrah Federal Building had already arrived at work and children had already been dropped off at the daycare center when the huge explosion tore through the building at 9:02 AM Nearly the entire north face of the nine-story building was pulverized into dust and rubble. McVeigh was executed for this crime, and Terry Nichols received a twelve-year jail term for his participation.

This is the two-wrongs-trying-to-make-a-right again. One bad action does not necessitate another. If McVeigh felt strongly about Waco or whatever else, he had recourse. It might be slower and certainly less spectacular, but you cannot change a system or improve it by bombing buildings and harming innocent people.

This tour of hate crimes is not yet over. Every day one can pick up a newspaper and find evidence of crimes, but these acts of violence are the result of being a victim and a hater. These crimes are born out of the philosophy that someone must get even and that the perpetrators have no other recourse than to kill innocent people to get their message across. This behavior is in perfect synchronization with the increase in hate speech and personal attacks. Attacking policies is work; attacking a person or blaming the government is easy.

Sikh Slain after 9/11

Balbir Singh Sodhi was a Sikh. He wore a turban and a beard as part of his religious practice and belief. Sikhism is a gentle and tolerant religion; followers of Sikhism believe that all paths lead to God. Sodhi owned a convenience store in Mesa, Arizona. Four days after 9/11, Sodhi was gunned down in front of his store by a man named Frank Roque. Roque was unaware that Sikhs are not Muslims and that the Sikh community had no ties to Islam or the attacks on the World Trade Center. The haters and victims had taken another life. The mental stereotype of what an Islamic terrorist looked like was not challenged, so a wrong identification was made. Mesa's Sikh community mourned the loss of Sodhi and is working to educate people about Sikhism to prevent further violence. It is good that they are trying to educate the community, but it and other communities must be willing to learn.

Hate Crimes against Muslims

The Council on American-Islamic Relations released a report in 2005 documenting anti-Muslim crimes and an increase in them. A mosque in Cincinnati was pipe-bombed. An elderly man leaving a mosque in Phoenix was attacked and beaten by a group of teenagers. In Virginia, a pregnant woman was assaulted by three men who shouted anti-Muslim slurs during the assault. Civil rights–related grievances by Muslims have risen drastically since 9/11. Discrimination, harassment, and violence against these people are up. The haters are at work, using the concept that every Muslim is a terrorist and every Muslim is a threat. There is no attempt to learn about the Islamic faith, just as there is seldom any attempt to learn about Judaism or Buddhism. Leaning about something is not sanctioning it or converting to it; it is about understanding it and practicing tolerance.

Shenandoah Hate Crime

Luis Ramirez came to the United States to work. He sought a better life, just as countless immigrants had done before. At the age of nineteen, he worked two jobs to support himself and his family in Mexico, working in factories, construction, and agriculture. He was in a committed relationship and the father of two young children. On the night of July12, 2009, a group of high school football players beat him to the ground, kicked him, stomped him, and then fractured his skull. He died as a result of this beating. During the assault, they shouted that he needed to go back to Mexico. A friend trying to come to his aid was told that all the Mexicans needed to get out of the Shenandoah Valley or the same thing would happen to them. The haters and victims are everywhere and in every age group.

Dissent

Somewhere in the recent past in the United States, dissent became bad and un-American. It is certain that the Founding Fathers would be baffled by this trend. While Eisenhower did promote the politics of consensus, he meant it as a tool to show the communists that we were united. This should not have been promoted in politics, and it certainly was not meant to apply to the general population. Dissent has some rules of order as well: you must defend someone else's right to speak and express a view to which you are antithetically opposed. America is not easy on this point, but freedom of speech means freedom of *all* speech. So while I called out Limbaugh, Hannity, Savage, and Beck because of the poison they spread, I do not deny them their right to speech. I find their negativity to be like a poison and so I do as I was taught to do, I turn them off. I do not buy their books; I do not support their sponsors; and I hope that others would do the same. It is also essential for those who listen to them or read their books to hold them accountable for producing facts and not just biased opinion and sound bites. Sound bites are clever but they are also used to demonize, propagandize, distort, and prevaricate.

We need to remember that dissent is not bad. If it were, then if you do not agree with somebody, you are wrong. Once you are wrong, then I have someone to blame: The government is to blame. The school is to blame. The police officer is to blame. No one has to assume any responsibility for their actions because someone else can be seen as responsible. Someone else caused our bad decisions, our debt, and our ignorance. We claim that no one told us. We ignore current events, call all media biased, and support causes that are themselves purveyors of hate.

It is easy to wrap ourselves in the flag and play some patriotic ditty. It is easy to explain that maybe someone tried to tell us but we were too busy to listen and understand. We live for sound bites and factoids. Our knowledge of the real issues is limited but that is someone else's fault. We complain about not being told the truth and about secret agendas, but we do not seek truth. We allow lobbyists to influence our lawmakers because we do not engage in the process, and anything left unmonitored is bound to run amok. We do not verify the data that is presented, and we do not evaluate sources for accuracy and bias. Numbers never lie, but liars always use numbers.

Not only did our Founding Fathers recognize the value of dissent, they were themselves dissenters. Dissenting does not mean one is anti-American; dissent does not mean disloyalty or subversion. Dissent means the expression of opposing views. It also means that the tyranny of the majority that concerned Alexis de Tocqueville cannot mutate into the tyranny of the minority.

Terri Schiavo

On March 31, 2005, Terri Schiavo died. This woman's case took on epic proportions in the press. Right-to-lifers inserted themselves into a case and a decision that should have been private and that clearly belonged to her family. That was part of the problem: the family included her husband and her parents. According to the media, Terri had been on a severe diet, causing a potassium deficiency. She went into a coma, and for twelve years the members of her family waited for her to wake up and join them again. Terri was declared brain dead, but her parents simply would not believe the medical evidence; instead they declared the husband unfit, manipulative, and a liar. Vigils were held, names were called, strangers came into the picture, lawyers were hired, and the slander of the husband was blatant.

On March 18, 2005, the feeding tubes were ordered removed and on March 31 Terri died. I hope she is able to rest in peace. After all the vilification, press, name-calling, slander, and hate, it is difficult to know who all the victims were, but certainly Terri was one, being kept on life support for twelve years with no hope of recovery. I also believe that her husband was a victim. He said she had died years earlier, and after the autopsy was performed it was confirmed that she had indeed been brain dead and that the motions that some had claimed indicated recognition were reflexive. I understand that her parents loved her and did not want to lose her, but to put her, her husband, and themselves through this was a high price to pay. Of course, it was also the media that brought out the haters and victims. In the name of news, we made this tragedy a media circus. I do not blame the press; they are only doing what we want them to do, which is to sensationalize every event and use the language that lobs bombs and presses the buttons of emotional hate and victimhood.

The Bridge Out of
New Orleans

The bridge to Gretna, Louisiana, was a major topic for the program *60 Minutes* in 2005. It was one of the few ways out of New Orleans after Hurricane Katrina blew into the Mardi Gras city. This particular bridge is called the Crescent City Connection, linking New Orleans with the west bank of the Mississippi River. Thousands of people had started to walk across the bridge on Wednesday; some made it across by bus in the hope of being in a better place. On Thursday, a group of tourists who had been staying in the French Quarter and some locals started across the bridge. Gretna police officers blocked their way, fired shotguns over their heads, and told them Gretna was closed. While the majority of people were black, there were some other races represented.

The police chief said he just could not figure out how to help any more people than had already arrived, but most believe the reason for halting their leaving New Orleans was racially motivated. The words and methods used to keep this group from crossing the bridge would indicate that the people who claimed bias were correct.

It is difficult to read intent and motives into a situation like this, but what is clear is that New Orleans was not going to be livable for most people for a very long time and the people stranded there needed to go elsewhere. In the case of the tourists, they wanted to go home, and Gretna would have been the start of the exodus to other areas. No one died from this incident but the impression of those who tried to cross the bridge was that the haters were on the other side.

Michael Vick

I do not know Michael Vick. The only association I have with him is that I have watched him play football. I was appalled at the crime for which he pleaded guilty. I do not condone mistreatment of animals, and while I do not even own a dog, I would never want any dog to be trained for fighting and then killed if it did not perform viciously enough. So what would put Michael's name in this small tome? Michael was charged and found guilty and sentenced to prison. He served his time. He lost his job. He apologized. He was censured by the NFL. He did community service. Still the voices would not be stilled.

He has already done more penance and restitution than some who have severely injured or murdered humans, but this is not enough. Some would have him homeless and unemployed for the rest of his life. He is taunted by people who think he was not punished enough. I hope Michael is able to make a life for himself again. He made a mistake, but it is time for the static to die down and let him start his life anew. Somehow we cannot ever let wrongdoings go, and we resent someone who tries to start over. He is currently playing for the Philadelphia Eagles, but there was heated controversy over his hiring and there is still controversy at every game.

Even as I finish this work, Tiger Woods, an exceptional golfer, is now the media focus. He has lived with discrimination all his life, yet has still excelled at his game. I care about Tiger because of his golf. Whatever else that has occurred is between him and his wife. He needs to get back to being a golfer, but as long as the media is creating a shark-feeding frenzy around him, this will not happen.

Company Lawsuits

Companies across the country have a bevy of lawyers working for them. There are tax attorneys, labor law attorneys, and liability attorneys. Any company with a liability policy will tell you that it is constantly being sued. Foreign objects in food, sometimes put there by the litigant; slip-and-fall injuries when there was no hazard; and defective parts when there were none: these are some of the tools used in the victims' scenarios.

These lawsuits make it much more difficult for those who actually are injured, because their legitimate suits get put in the same stack as the made-up ones. Between a nation of litigants (victims) and a nation of haters, it is difficult to tell the good guys from the bad ones. It is even more difficult for a company to recover its reputation and goodwill in the face of all the misinformation that passes for facts these days. Sometimes companies may indeed be at fault for something but many are just deep pockets for the victims and haters who cannot figure out how to make a living any other way.

By the way, not everyone is discriminated against. Some people are just not qualified or competent. Some people may be good writers, or accountants, or sales personnel but cannot transition to other positions and still be effective. The concept of rising to your own level of mediocrity is still a factor. This is not the message people want to hear, so lawsuits and the threat of them are ever present.

Just look at the number of lawyers we have in this country. According to statistics published in 2006, there is approximately one lawyer for every thirty-six Americans. France has one lawyer for 1,313 people. Japan has one lawyer for 5,790 and China has one for every million people. If this is not a data point giving hard evidence of our victimhood, I can think of few others that would. While many attorneys are not in the victim compensation mode, TV ads are crowded with examples of those who make a living convincing people that they are victims.

The Language of Hate

We use language to communicate, explain, sell, and describe. There are many languages spoken worldwide and some, like body language, are nonverbal. Language can soothe, inflame, quiet, and direct. The words used can be positive or negative, right or wrong. John Adams wrote, "Abuse of words has been the great instrument of sophistry and chicanery, of party, faction, and division of society." Our current events are littered with an abuse of words.

It could probably be argued that the language of hate began when we first developed speech. The valley people whose crops failed blamed the mountain people because the valley people worshipped the river and the mountain people worshipped the sun and they needed someone to blame for their failed crops. The other people, the different people, were the cause of the problem. In order to make this hate work, a language for hate was developed. Stereotyping people feeds this language of hate. Name-calling is part of the language of hate. Phrases such as "those people" and "fat cats" are examples of the language of hate, even though they contain no expletives. There is a tradition in Western religions in which God blames humans for making a mess of things, so the blame game can permeate everything we do, if we let it. Jesus Christ was the ultimate victim of this blame game, yet Christian teachings are corrupted in the psychology of many Americans. We are willing to use Christianity to explain our hate, our prejudice, and our bigotry. Some even point to passages in the Bible that prove that their negative and irrational thinking is justified in dealing with others.

We use many words to evoke emotions and those emotions cause hate and fear and tension. We use words like immigrant, black, white, old, poor, welfare and unemployed. Of course we change these words into something more visceral, and just the act of using negative and derogatory words makes us feel better and more powerful. We also use words to divide us. We allow ourselves to be categorized: red states, blue states, Republican, Democrat, radical, liberal, and fanatic. We listen to people who let us know how we are different from others and how we are being injured by them. We toss around terms like socialism and communism as if we actually understood what they meant. We insult our neighbors in Canada and our friends in Europe.

If you want facts, you will not find them anywhere this dialogue is taking place. Yes, socialism is a form of government and it must work somewhere: France, England, Australia, Austria, Germany, and Canada, to name a few. I am pretty sure the citizens of those countries are surprised to find out how vehemently we hate them and their governments. Some of us have traveled there and certainly enjoyed the visit, but we would not want to live somewhere that allows six weeks of vacation; milk money to new mothers; monitored, licensed, and, in some cases, subsidized daycare so parents can have safe places for their children; and health care open twenty-four hours a day, seven days a week. That might be way too radical for our independent and capitalist tastes.

The language of hate must be couched in words and phrases that make it hard for people to distinguish the blowhards and the simpleminded from the fact givers. The haters use one of the oldest tricks in the book: fallacies, arguments that are not logically valid. Fallacies are used to mislead and misdirect the thoughts of others. If a distorted idea has a kernel of truth and can generate megawatts of emotion, it is a successful fallacy—but that does not make it true.

Fallacies are used repeatedly in the press and in political rhetoric. No one corrects them, so once again, if you tell a lie often enough it becomes the truth. Lloyd Bentsen had a great sound bite during a vice presidential debate against Dan Quayle. "I knew Jack Kennedy. Jack Kennedy was a friend of mine. Senator, you are no Jack Kennedy." While I certainly agreed with Mr. Bentsen, the issue was not Kennedy, and he was attacking Quayle and not the issues. This is an ad hominem fallacy, which means attacking the man, but many other kinds of fallacies exist: appeal to emotion, appeal to popularity, red herrings, appeal to authority, and many more.

Repeating how much money is wasted, or misused, or misspent is also frequently a fallacy. It is important to recognize that such fallacies exist and how often they are used. It is not that money is never misused or wasted, but we should stop blaming the government and start prosecuting the crooks who do the real misdeeds.

The media repeatedly use the appeal-to-authority fallacy. Wilford Brimley hawks diabetic supplies and Charles Barkley hawks deodorant. They do this well but it is not because they have any great insight into the products. It is a case of if I told you something was cheaper or that one product worked better than another, you would want to know if I could prove it, but it is assumed that a celebrity who is paid for the endorsement must know something. I have nothing against endorsements as long as people are aware that the hawkers are not experts.

We talk about entitlements and entitlements are welfare—everyone knows that. This is also a logical fallacy; it is an argument from popular opinion. Somewhere in time, programs like Social Security became entitlement programs because when they started there was no money in the federal coffers to pay for the programs. That changed. Every working American who receives a W-2 pays into Social Security, as does their employer. This tax collection has been so successful that for many years there was a surplus. Since 1981, at least $60 billion has been taken from the Social Security Trust Fund annually to pay for things such as the Strategic Defense Initiative, the first Persian Gulf War, paying down the national debt, and funding the Iraq and Afghanistan operations. These withdrawals add up to over $1 trillion. We cannot lock the barn door after the animals have fled, but we certainly can require accountability for those funds and demand the trust fund not be raided anymore.

The topic of abortion also breeds the language of hate. Let us be clear; there is no one in this country—absolutely no one—who advocates abortion. There is a chasm of difference between having the right to something and advocating something. In all my years, no one has ever knocked on my door and asked if I wanted an abortion. If they had that would be advocating for abortions.

I am a self-declared pro-life, pro-choice person. I have been told I cannot be both and my reply is, "of course I can and so can others." If you ask me what I would do, I choose life. I believe that life is a gift, and I am grateful for every day I wake up because each day is a gift for me. I am pro-choice because I refuse to make that same decision for others. Our society has developed in such a way that in spite of rhetoric about family values and morals, we have not created the social support systems to actually be family friendly. Churches fail to support young women who become pregnant when single, and these women are branded as sinful. In the past they had to be separated from the good girls. If women felt they had support systems and daycare and whatever it would take to raise their children, abortion would be the least attractive option for them to choose.

Women should not be forced to have a child they cannot raise or cannot love. Adoption could be made a more viable option if the courts supported the anonymity of the mother if she desired it and if the rights of adoptive parents were upheld. Instead, we use terms like baby-killers and murderers for women who have an abortion and the doctors who terminate pregnancies. I am sure that I could find equally ugly names for those who would deny women their right to make this decision for themselves, but instead I believe we need to recognize the language of hate, the climate of violence, and the double standard that is allowed to permeate the population. This double standard is the concept that it is okay for the haters and victims to fill the airwaves with their grievances but those who choose to research facts and disseminate truth are supposed to remain silent. This double standard is also that we will not help families prosper while we talk about family values. This double standard is advocating against abortion but not providing support to young women who need it if they do not have one.

This language of hate even applies to the current economic crisis. "Bailout" has become an evil word that evokes hateful diatribes. When the topic comes up, I have insisted that people tell me whether the money was a loan or a gift. A loan implies we will get the money back. A gift means that the money goes into a black hole and is never seen again, much like when grown children ask for a "loan." The money authorized by Congress was predominantly a loan. It is expected that much of these funds will be repaid, and some already has been. Let us begin to demand that the right language be used so that those still tied to sound bites hear it correctly each time.

The current economic crisis also has shown how many of us have grown into haters and victims. Homeowners who scammed the system and bought homes that they knew they could not qualify for under other circumstances took advantage of loopholes and shoddy mortgage lending practices. "Those people" made victims out of all of us. Bernie Madoff created another set of victims. Of course, many victims do not acknowledge that they were also part of the problem and what they were sold was too good to be true and that there is no such thing as a free lunch. It seems that some bought into get-rich-quick schemes and did not want to know how things were being done. If it seems too good to be true, it is not true.

In a nation obsessed with being "haves," the details of how that might happen were not required. I am truly sorry they lost money in this Ponzi scheme or that scam, but somewhere in the investment or the mortgage process a warning bell should have gone off. Perhaps the desire for wealth caused them to ignore the bell. We must be willing to ask the tough questions and get the right answers before we invest our life savings. We must make sure that there are controls in place to warn us if something goes awry.

There are people in this country who do not want health-care reform simply because it means that people with health-care benefits will no longer subsidize those who do not have them. Every person with health-care benefits pays a premium that, in addition to their own coverage, covers some of the losses that doctors and hospitals, especially emergency rooms, accrue because of the patients who do not have coverage and cannot afford to pay for their treatment.

I am not an expert in health care, but I do have more than my share of common sense. We need to fix health care and we need to fix it now. Procrastination and fearful rhetoric designed to inflame people are obvious in Congress. The haters are so good at this they had to bus people into the town hall meetings just to show everyone else how uninformed and lacking in trust we seem to be. A nation as economically developed as we are should not rank 45 in the infant mortality tables (and this fact came from our own CIA Factbook).

There are people in this country who use the language of hate to make people believe they are being taken advantage of in any reform plan: "Illegals" will be covered by the plan. There will be waste and fraud if the government sponsors a health-care plan Does this imply there is never waste and fraud if the government is not involved? Names like Enron, MCI WorldCom, Best Choice Medical Services, Qwest, Aspen, Broadcom, Spectrum, Adelphia, Dell, Cendant, and AIG come to mind as recent and real examples of fraud and misdeeds—and the government was not involved.

We talk about quotas and reverse discrimination as if all of us, whoever "we" are, are the victims. We have passed propositions to prohibit tax increases in California, which have crippled the state. California needs more electric power, but vocal minorities have made sure that there is little opportunity for new power plants; and so the crippling continues. I would posit that most of the people who vote for the laws that are passed don't understand them, and now they are doubly confused because the system has failed and no one seems to have the moxie to fix it.

In the 1950s, *Life* magazine did a graphic pictorial of the violence committed against blacks in the South. Readers were disturbed and appalled. Torture, beatings, lynchings, and terror were present in the photographs. The reasons for this behavior seemed unfathomable, yet these were once again the deeds of victims and haters. The pictures of the haters and victims lining the walkways to the high school in Little Rock during the forced desegregation made the hate palpable.

In the 1960s and 1970s, it seemed we blamed the soldiers who served in Vietnam instead of the Congress that sent them. In the 1970s, it was Nixon who caused all our problems with the economy and Watergate. Then it was Ford's fault for pardoning Nixon and being clumsy. Then it was Carter's fault because he was seeking peace in the Middle East but did not understand the culture of victims and haters and did not know that the Beltway is populated with scavengers and vultures who feed the victims and haters. In the 1980s, it was big business: break up AT&T, deregulate airlines and trucking, and bust up unions. The victims and haters were told that these groups were the cause of their problems and that they were being cheated and overcharged; therefore, these industries must change or go so Americans can be more competitive and we can keep jobs here. Did anyone notice this did not happen?

In the 1990s, it was Iraq and Saddam Hussein, and then 9/11 occurred and it is again Iraq and Afghanistan. We cannot forget, however, that it is also Somalia, North Korea, Iran, and Venezuela. Ask yourself why South Africans went to the polls and elected a man with strong communist leanings, or why the people of Venezuela elected Hugo Chavez. The reason is that they appeal to the fear in people and they tell their voters who the cause of their problems is and how they are going to fix it (whatever it is). It little matters if they fix it; instead everyone knows who is to blame for the problem, and it is not the person elected. Perhaps they convince their constituents that they feel their pain. In the United States, we have yet another group that blames liberals for the decline in morality and blames rap for promoting violence.

Family values have been a concern of governments since at least the fifth century BCE. Socrates was accused of corrupting the minds of the youth of Athens and, because he refused exile, was forced to commit suicide. To set this record straight, all families have values. Most families only want the best for each other, including health and prosperity. These items are currently out of reach for many Americans. This hot button called family values is just another smoke screen erected to tell you how bad things are and how everyone else is in decline, but it never applies to you personally.

If you want to know where your job went, look to the tax breaks given to companies in the 1980s for off-shoring. Our then very popular president said we needed to be more competitive. Americans were then and still are the most productive workers on the planet but we have lost motivation and desire because we have lost our sense of security. We have off-shored most steel mills, electronics, textiles, car manufacturing (except for some assembly plants), call centers, and information technology support. Many research and development jobs as well as engineers have been off-shored. We even off-shore passport creation to Thailand. We don't have much left. So exactly how the world's richest economy will continue to be the richest is a great question. One of the reasons our current crisis is so dire is that we had already off-loaded millions of jobs and there is nothing to fall back on in our current time of troubles. We are uncertain, insecure, and confused, and we do not understand, but the haters and victims do not have the answers to our questions. We have continued to root for the little guy and given to others around the world when needed. We have made great progress, and we should not let the haters and victims stop our progress.

We will know when we are not giving in to the language of hate. We will know because we will stop describing our president as black or the new Supreme Court justice as a Latina and a woman. We will have actually gone over to the light when we can stop celebrating Black History Month because now we are teaching American history—all American history—and teaching it accurately and truthfully. Our history should be an honest retelling of our story, warts and all. We have done many despicable and deplorable things over the past three hundred years, yet we have also created a nation that did what no other nation had done before: break from our mother country and forge a new nation. This nation is a republic, a democratic republic, and its citizens have rights and freedoms. Along with our pride in this nation we need to make sure we learn from its history. We cannot ignore its lessons or all that we have strived for and so many have died for will indeed be for nothing.

The Final Chapter

I would be remiss if I only diagnosed the disease and offered no cures. It is not too late. We can reverse this trend of victimhood and hate. We can be informed and educated. We can gain an informed opinion, not one based on sound bites and misinformation. We can research the facts instead of believing chain e-mails and slanted surveys. We can ask questions: "Is that true?" "How do you *know* that?" "How were those numbers compiled?" These should all be part of our daily vernacular. If you want to take your country back, you can start by being an informed voter and make sure you vote on not just one issue but on all issues. You should understand that some information is biased and what the bias is. I would also posit that your country does not need to be taken back; the way we think about our country needs to be improved.

We must bring civics, world history, and geography back to our classrooms. We must educate people in the United States on the Constitution, the Bill of Rights, and what citizens' rights and responsibilities are. People should be able to name the fifty states and the state capitals. We need to teach geography and world history so we learn what the world is all about. People should know where Chad is or what the capital of Libya is. If we want to be competitive in the future, we must learn about the world and cultures that are different from our own. Companies all over America are working on diversity initiatives, but in most minds the idea of diversity is still vested in color and gender. Diversity is also diversity of thought. Some of our best technology companies have reaped the benefits of this type of diversity, and this is a positive example of how well things can work when we are pulling together for common goals.

Americans need to know that they (we) are the government. Governments are formed by people to benefit the people who formed them. We do not have a democracy in the United States; we have a democratic republic. A republic by definition is a representative form of government, and it is our responsibility to know exactly who we elect to represent us. The president can have a legislative agenda but the president cannot pass laws single-handledly. There are 100 senators and 435 representatives who can.

Congress should not be passing petty legislation that has appeal only to a vocal minority. Although they are not elected on a national level (only the president and vice president are elected nationally), Congress has a say in everything that occurs nationally. Americans should hold them responsible for what they say and the laws they introduce or vote for or against. Do not berate them for working on legislation, but make your voice heard. This is the stuff that makes a democratic republic work year after year and allows for the peaceful transition of power from one president to another. Just as our government is representative, so should the feedback be representative, not only coming from a vocal minority.

There is much good information out there, although somehow it does not have the broad-based appeal of reality television. But what could present more reality then the History Channel, the Military History Channel, and the Discovery Channel? Public broadcasting stations have some of the best programs available and they cross all the genres from children's programming to science and business news. This is a source of balanced programming that is overlooked. National Public Radio and public television are underfunded, but that makes sense because these stations and programs are the antithesis of ignorance. Even if you disagree with the material presented, at least someone is presenting it.

Americans need to read books. It is irrelevant whether they're on a Kindle or listened to on an MP3 player. There should be a required reading list for all Americans. Ideas should be shared and explored. Books have the power to inspire and motivate. Americans should read *Common Sense* by Thomas Paine, the Declaration of Independence, and the Patriot Act. We should read mystery books, books by Shakespeare, poems, science fiction, and the epics—*The Iliad, Beowulf, The Odyssey, and The Aeneid*. Tolstoy, Marx, Salinger, Frost, Sandburg, Rand,

Bradbury, Russell, Plato, Twain, and Melville should all be required reading. We do not have to agree with everything we read, but exposure to ideas prepares us for thinking from a position of knowledge and strength, not from the position of being a hater and a victim and weak.

Remember always that the United States is not a homogenous culture. As a nation of immigrants, we are diverse and different, yet all of us are Americans. It is irrelevant whether we are black, white, yellow, brown, red, Catholic, Protestant, Jewish, Muslim, Mormon, fat, thin, red-haired, blonde, tall, short, or whether we eat perogies or hummus. The strength of this country is that we are diverse, and if we play to this strength we have ensured the continuation of our nation and culture. We should sample all this immigrant society has to offer and learn from the experience, whether a seder or a church festival or a taste of what so many cities sponsor. This is how we break down the barriers and build bridges.

Intolerance leads to destruction. Every nation that declared a state religion in the past has fallen. If we learn from history we will recognize this fact. Greece, Rome, the British Empire, France, and others all fell. I can tell you that the government in Iran will fall. I cannot tell you when, but history tells me it is so. Intolerance causes the failure of nations, so we need to change the behavior of the victims and haters and make sure they do not succeed where others have failed.

We need to bring back a balance in this country. We have lost the yin and yang of things. We need to balance industry, business, manufacturing, farming, services, mining, steel, textiles, and the environment. We need jobs. Americans need to ensure their livelihoods; when they feel their paychecks are threatened, they become part of the legion of victims and haters. The cycle is complete, but not on a positive note.

Deregulation, cuts in social programs, and two wars have taken their toll on the country. Illiteracy rates are growing. Everyone missed the growing number of jobs being outsourced, and then our self-inflicted economic crisis hit. This double whammy led to even higher unemployment and the inability of employment numbers to recover quickly. We've seen reductions in benefits, lack of health-care coverage, and lack of funding for public defenders and psychiatric facilities. The No Child Left Behind policy has left many children behind all across the country. In some cases. teachers are teaching to the test and not teaching for long-term learning. Constant playing on the fears generated by the 9/11 attacks has altered our collective consciousness and exacerbated our insecurities. People blame everyone except those who reap the benefits of our current financial and social order. Many of these problems go back twenty or thirty years, but because the root cause is not acknowledged, the cure is harder to find.

This nation does have real problems and I am not qualified to speak to all of them, but I am sure that a nation of haters and victims cannot prosper. I am sure that if we continue to spend more time worrying about how Michael Jackson died than we do learning what is happening in the world—and asking how the United States can possibly influence things if it cannot prosper—we have the wrong focus.

If we want to take back this country, we must value education. We must go to school, make our children go to school, hold the school systems responsible for educating, and hold our representatives responsible for the work they do. I am not advocating reneging on our promises to other countries, but we have spent billions of borrowed dollars in Iraq. That money could have been used to rebuild our education infrastructure, fix our social programs, and increase our national security. It could also have created some of the jobs we need. If national security requires this then so be it, but if the dust ever settles over Iraq and Afghanistan then we need to make sure we fix what is broken here as well.

We should require and expect facts, not stories and myths. We must make sure that we are not guilty of what we most dislike in others. Legislators do not always have to pass laws you fully agree with, but they must vote their consciences, not how some lobbyist who has more influence than you told them to vote. Edmund Burke, a member of the British parliament before the American Revolution, said: "Your representative owes you, not his industry only, but his judgment; and he betrays instead of serving you if he sacrifices it to your opinion."

Burke also wrote, "All that is necessary for the triumph of evil is for good men to do nothing." We have good people in this country. We have ordinary, honest, and decent people in this country. We have hard-working, hopeful, joyful, pleasant, and optimistic people. The circumstances of the last several years have made it difficult for these good qualities to take center stage, but there are still plenty of Americans who love this country as much as I do and who want to be proud of being American again. For some, ugly rhetoric and manipulative jargon have taken them down a dark and foreboding path. We do not want to be thought of or remembered as purveyors of hate. Walter Cronkite was one of the most respected journalists of the twentieth century, and he was not guilty of conveying hate and victimhood with every breath.

We must think. We must care. We must vote. We must hold ourselves and others accountable. We need to begin tuning out the haters. Those who see a conspiracy behind every word or deed and who only know how to tear down, not build up, must be muted by our own indifference to their venom and illogic. Only when we stand together as Americans will we defeat those who want us to fail.

If you need to turn the dogs loose, loose them on the greed of those who find loopholes in the law and cause misery to investors and pensioners. Loose the dogs on those who want to divide us, because divided we will be conquered. Loose the dogs on the crooks, the cheats, the liars, and the unlawful. Loose the dogs on the haters and those who would make us victims. I am not advocating attacking them and making them martyrs and victims but starving them of audiences they are not worthy of nor deserve to have.

We do not need to support those who preach the gospel of hate, but we should support those who are trying to fix what is broken. I am not advocating violence but behavioral changes. We must reject those who continually tell us how bad something is but offer nothing in its place. We must recognize that citizens in each state elect senators and representatives but all voters elect the president, and we only have one president at a time. We should be proud of the fact that every four or eight years we have a peaceful transition of government and there are no tanks patrolling our cities. We can ensure that the terrorists and those mired in cupidity do not prosper.

We can recover from this disease that permeates our lives and fills the airwaves. We need the media to report news and not make the news into a daily soap opera or reality TV show. Broadcasters should be held to a standard of performance that means they report facts and tell us what happened, not what they want us to think happened.

We can admit that we have fallen prey to the incendiary nature of haters and victims. We can take the pledge today to ask for, demand if we must, the facts. We are not powerless; nor are we spineless. Americans have been tested in the past and we have passed the test many times. Negativity breeds more negativity; it is easier to complain than compliment these days. We focus on the teenager who shot someone more than on the teenagers who volunteered at the food bank or donated their spending money to the Salvation Army. The news has nothing to say about the many volunteer organizations with volunteers young and old working to make a difference. Our media should report what is known and stop the speculation that, once uttered, becomes fact in people's minds.

We have the talent and ability to overcome our problems and make the nation stronger than ever before. We do have serious problems, but we will not resolve them by being afraid, screaming at each other, and slamming the doors shut. The greatest challenge to our democratic republic is our unwillingness to learn from each other, listen to each other, and work with each other.

Building a wall between the United States and Mexico might make someone feel good, but walls have never kept people out or in. Even the poet Robert Frost noted that there is something about walls that leads people to bring them down. The Berlin Wall is a classic example of just such a wall. If we want to stop illegal immigration, let us actually have a foreign policy with Mexico that helps them build their industries and allows Mexican workers to be employed at living wages. This is what we want and why most of our ancestors came here. We can build walls—or bridges.

Another controversy exists around the concept of law mandating English as the official language and not allowing citizenship unless English is spoken. If it is the national will that English be the language of the land, we need to pass the laws to enforce this. This is not discrimination. If the requirements for citizenship and visas clearly state that English is our spoken language, we must be brave enough to pass this legislation. This topic is one that the haters and victims drag out at every opportunity, so put it to a national referendum and let voters vote, as a democratic process allows. Other countries have enacted legislation about their official languages, and we could also, but that might not be in the best interest of some of the special interest groups. As a nation we need to decide what our national character is and what it will be. We can be inclusive or exclusive. We can claim homogeneity but actually be heterogeneous. We can be Americans in name only or actually be Americans. Nothing worth doing is ever easy, and although we should not expect easy or quick fixes to our problems, we must have solutions.

The world has changed. It has become perceptively smaller and harder to understand. Suicide bombers, changing economies, climate concerns, wars that drain our resources but are not winnable—all are areas of concern, and not just for us. The world shares these concerns. Addressing these issues requires leadership. We should stop looking for the perfect plan, however, because we will never please everyone. General Patton, who had a bias toward action, once remarked that a good plan today is better than a perfect plan tomorrow. We should also have a bias toward action. We can make a difference and we can stop the flow of hate. Take the pledge and help rebuild our national psyche. Just so no to haters and victims.

The resilience of the American people is incredible. The Revolutionary War, the War of 1812, the Civil War, two world wars, depressions, recessions, oil shortages, terrorist attacks, Watergate, spies, and hurricanes have failed to stymie our spirits or thwart our progress. This country has a historic pioneer spirit and the modern-day entrepreneurial talent to weather any crisis and come out ahead. This has not been done with hand-wringing and negativity but with ideas, creations, innovations, open minds, and possibilities.

One of our Founding Fathers, John Adams, said, "There are only two creatures of value on the face of the earth: those with the commitment, and those who require the commitment of others." We must have this commitment and require others to share it with us. It is time we took back our country, but with the knowledge that education and research bring us. We can be like Diogenes of ancient Greece and carry a lamp, looking for an honest man, or more practically we can be honest and hold others to the same standards of honesty. The truth does not just set us free; it will keep us free.

References

http://answers.google.com/answers/threadview/id/2638.htm

http://www.ajhs.org/publications/chapters/chapter.cfm?documentID=284

http://americanhistory.si.edu/Brown/history/6-legacy/freedom-struggle-2.html

http://www.brainyquote.com/quotes/authors/e/edmund_burke_6.html

http://www.brainyquote.com/quotes/authors/e/edmund_burke.html

http://www.cbsnews.com/stories/200/12/15/60minutes/main1129440.shtml

http://www.cnn.com/US/9902/22/dragging.death.03/

http://www.cnn.com/2005/LAW/03/31/schiavo/index.html

http://www.core-online.org/History/freedom%20rides.htm

www.eastvalleytribune.com/story/74116 -www.hispanicvista.com/hvc/coliminst/misc/0051509maldef.htm

http://www.history.com/this-day-in-history.do?action=article&id=5088

http://www.history.com/minisite.do?content_type=Minisite_Generic&content_type_id=57770&display_order=1&sub_display_order=6&mini_id=1071

http://www.eastvalleytribune.org/okc/okc.htm

http://news.bbc.co.uk/2/hi/americas/504215.stm

http://www.malcolmx.com

http://news.newsamericamedia.org/news/view_article.html?article_id = 127fe2880e48951b564ac2f3e171242e

http://www.merriam-webster.com/dictionary/war

http://plato.stanford.edu/entries/hobbes-moral

http://thinkexist.com/quotation/how_fortunate_for_governments_that_the_people/157631.html.

http://www.time.com/time/specials/2007/la_riot/article/0,28804,1614117_1614084_1614511,00.html.